from the *award-winning*
'RUBY'S STUDIO: THE FRIENDSHIP SHOW'

A LITTLE BOOK ABOUT
FRIENDSHIP

Written by: Samantha Kurtzman-Counter & Abbie Schiller
Based on a screenplay by: Ruby Vanderzee
Character Design/Illustration: Charlotte Blacker - *Book Design:* Rae Friis

Library of Congress Control Number: 2013939911
www.TheMotherCo.com

THE MOTHER
COMPANY

Friends are one of the *greatest* parts of life.

But **how does** friendship **work?**

To *make friends*, we say "Hi"
and introduce ourselves.

We choose friends because they're *interesting*, or *smart*, or *silly*, or because they're a lot of *fun* to be around.

Most of all, there's just something
we really *like* about them!

Kindness makes a friendship *stronger*.

When we are kind to our friends,
they *want* to be kind back!

Friends introduce us to *n e w t h i n g s*.

And friends share

Friends care about each other.

We listen to our *friends* when they are upset.

“AAAAAA
AAACCC
CCCCCCCHH
HHHH
HHHHOO
Oooooo
ooOOOOoo
OoOOOO
Ooo!”

AaaaaAAAAAaaaaaaaaaaaaaaaa

hhhh AhhAh h

HHHHHHh hhhhhhhhhhhhhhh!

17

Sometimes friends make mistakes.

When a friend is in need, we try to be helpful.

When our friends get *mad*, we work out our problems together.

It can *help* to use our words
with friends when we are *u p s e t*.

Saying "Sorry" can make a friend *feel* much better.

Forgiveness shows our friends
we like and accept them, no matter what.

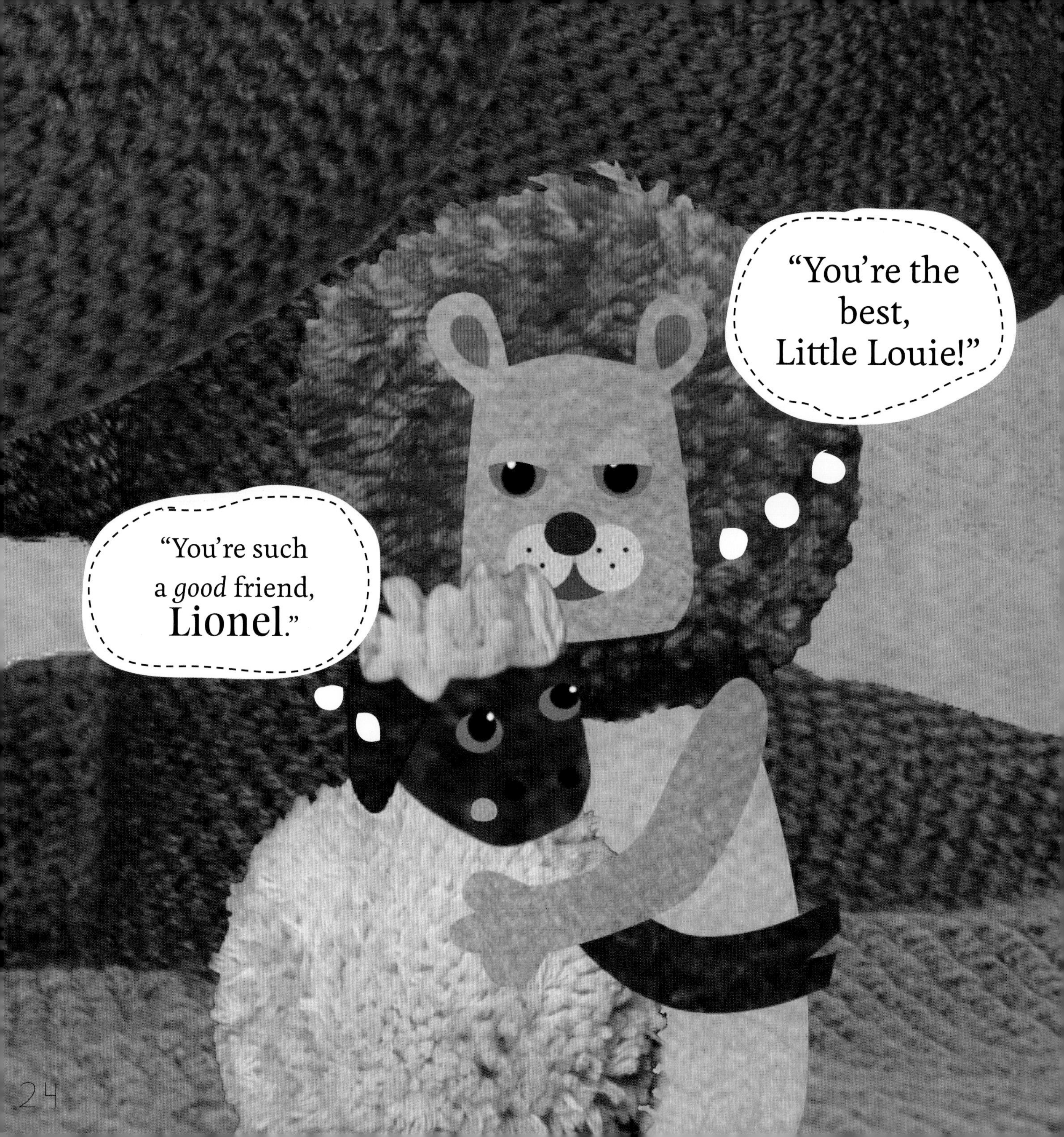
"You're the best, Little Louie!"
"You're such a *good* friend, Lionel."

• • • • • • • • • • • • • • • • • • • •

When friends are

nice

to us and we're

nice

to them, we become closer.

It feels great to have

g o o d

f r i e n d s .

• • • • • • • • • • • • • • • • • • • •

There are *so many* *wonderful* things about friendship. Friends fill our lives with…

LOVE.

A Note to Parents & Teachers

As parents and educators, teaching children about the importance of friendship is one of the most valuable lessons we can impart. Research repeatedly shows that having successful relationships in early childhood leads to a higher quality of life throughout adulthood. Friendships take work and commitment, flexibility and understanding — and the payoff is huge. By nurturing healthy friendships, children feel a growing sense of belonging and security as they learn how to communicate, empathize, resolve conflicts, and explore new horizons they never imagined before.

However, the ability to make and nurture strong friendships is a learned skill, not an inborn trait. *A Little Book About Friendship* helps young children understand the purpose and benefit of friendship by answering some essential questions: why have friends? How does friendship work? How does it make life better, sweeter, more expansive, and fun? Lionel the Lion and Louie the Sheep find each other on the playground and learn some pretty important friendship skills together: they introduce each other to new things, and they practice sharing, caring, understanding, problem solving and forgiveness. This unlikely pair offers young kids helpful tools to build strong, lasting friendships in a gentle, relatable way.

Here at The Mother Company, we aim to support parents, teachers, and caregivers by exploring the social and emotional obstacles young children face every day. With *A Little Book About Friendship*, we hope to inspire a helpful early dialogue about friendship in order to set the stage for healthy relationships throughout our children's lives.

— *Abbie Schiller and Sam Kurtzman-Counter, The Mother Company Mamas*

Guided by the mission to "Help Parents Raise Good People," The Mother Company offers world-renowned expert advice for parents at TheMotherCo.com, as well as the "Ruby's Studio" line of award-winning products for children.

THE MOTHER COMPANY

Hi, I'm Ruby!
What's your name?

RUBY'S STUDIO

Social & Emotional Learning For Kids

HELPFUL, FUN, AWARD-WINNING PRODUCTS

Enriching Books

Videos

Mobile Apps & eBooks

Toys & Activities

LEARN MORE AT RUBYsSTUDIO.COM

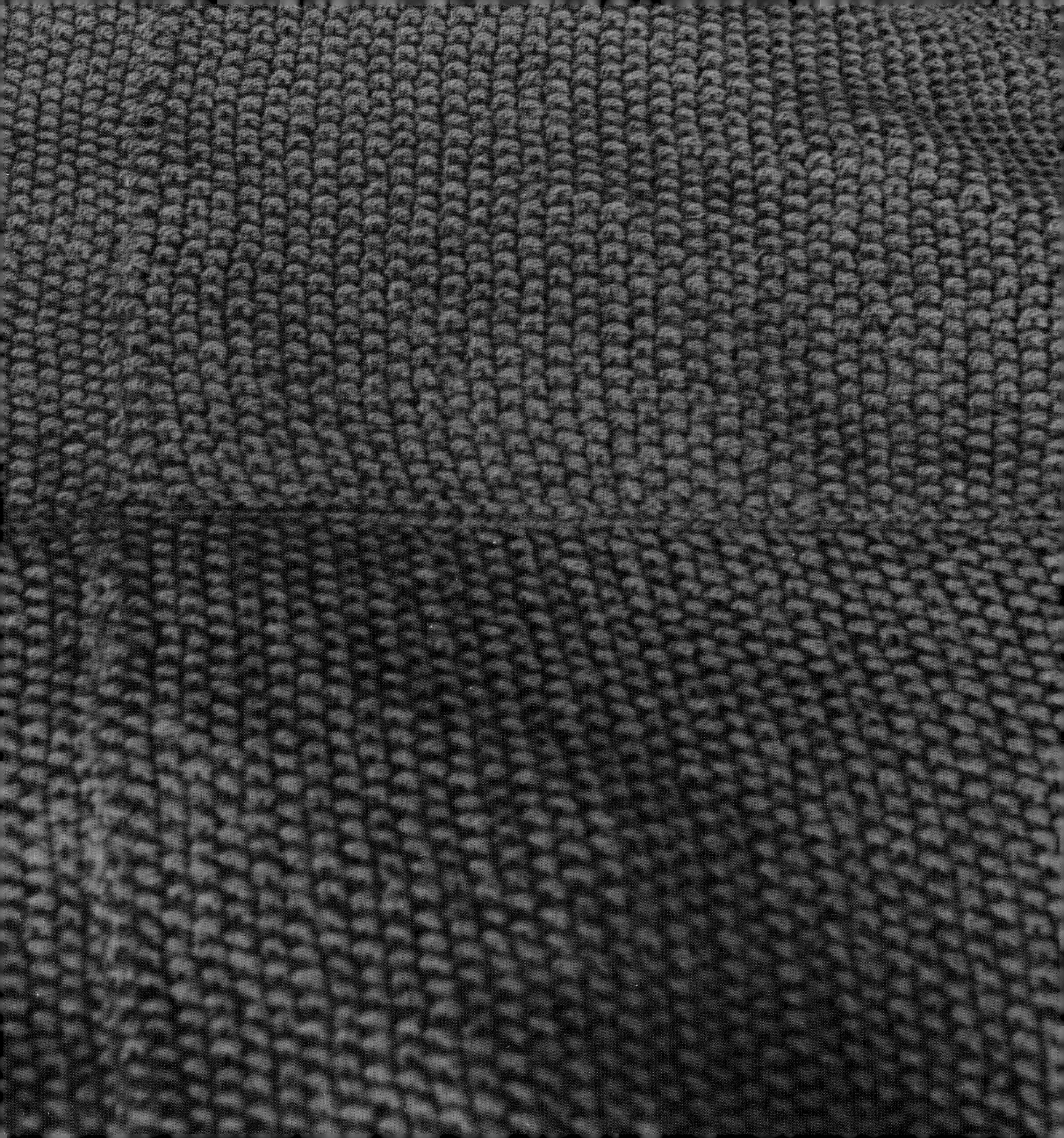